WASHINGTON'S KKK

Produced in the Republic of South Carolina by
SHOTWELL PUBLISHING LLC
Post Office Box 2592
Columbia, So. Carolina 29202

www.ShotwellPublishing.com

ISBN-13: 978-0692718179
ISBN- 0692718176

10 9 8 7 6 5 4 3 2 1

WASHINGTON'S KKK

THE UNION LEAGUE
During Southern Reconstruction

By John Chodes

Foreword by Dr. Clyde N. Wilson

CONTENTS

FOREWORD

OF THE DISTORTIONS OF AMERICAN HISTORY that have gained dominance in our time of Political Correctness, none is more extreme than the interpretation of Reconstruction. Reconstruction was once viewed as a destructive period of oppression and corruption fueled by greed and hate. The current official version of Reconstruction is that there was a reign of terror--- systematic murder and intimidation by the "white Southern ruling class," determined to keep the black people in virtual slavery. This is the Marxist class conflict formula for history, today known as Political Correctness. This interpretation and its categories have little basis in reality.

The real picture is a good deal more complicated. One can find plenty of material about conflict, intimidation, and killing in America in the period 1865–1877. But the PC school take for granted as fact what is clearly partisan propaganda from the time. In almost every case there is conflicting testimony or inadequate sources so that judgment becomes a matter of who you believe are the good guys and who are the bad guys. For the PC historians it is axiomatic that all violence is caused by reactionaries who are resisting the revolution, no matter who actually fires the first shot. This is standard Marxist doctrine.

They never ask the essential factual and moral question: who initiated violence?

Certainly the white people of the South did not want to live in a society dominated by their ex-slaves and outsiders and sometimes resorted to intimidation. Northerners would have done exactly the same in the same situation. Yet Reconstruction began with no overt hostility to the black people. In fact, the general attitude of most ex-Confederates right after the war was gratitude to the blacks who, after all, had for the most part remained loyal despite ample provocation and opportunity to do otherwise. Many prominent and influential Southerners like Robert E. Lee, Wade Hampton, and Bedford Forrest spoke of the wisdom, decent necessity, and long-range benefits in helping the black people to advance in their condition.

John Chodes shows that violence was begun by the Republicans. The Union League was an organisation that suppressed dissent in the North during the war and moved to the South with the mission of turning white Southerners into "good" Northerners--- in the process becoming a vigilante force. Its Southern operations consisted of secret meetings at night where black people were given promises and encouraged to assert dominance---and marshaled as voters to ensure permanent Republican control by illegitimate Carpetbag state governments. Armed black mobs (officially designated militia) led by Carpetbaggers roamed around intimidating, stealing, harassing, and murdering. They deliberately provoked violent response. And remember, their coercion was directed not only at whites but to any black people who refused to join. In other words, the Union League used the methods of the Ku Klux Klan before the Klan came into existence.

John Chodes is a distinguished playwright and biographer and a lifelong resident of New York City. He became interested in the War Between the States and Southern History after studying the U.S. Army's invasion and occupation of his city during the war. This led him to an important and neglected part of Reconstruction history---

the terrorist role of the Republican Union League. He tells us what really happened.

Clyde N. Wilson
Carolina, 2016

INTRODUCTION

THE NOTORIOUS KU KLUX KLAN was created in 1867 in Pulaski, Tennessee. Numerous groups claiming descent from the original organisation have existed and continue to exist today. Indeed, the name and deeds of the Klan continues to provoke fear, loathing, and the cry of "racism" whenever its name is evoked or its image is portrayed in Hollywood and elsewhere in the media.

The legend of the Klan and its "invisible empire" has also provided the Federal government with a golden opportunity to greatly expand its size and scope as it endlessly ferrets out real or imagined racists, not only in the South but in every corner of the United States.

Yet our comprehension of the Klan and its deeds is inverted.

It has been handed down to us for well over a century by Washington, DC. As the Confederate and United States Congressman, Jabez Curry said: "No conquered people ever wrote the accepted history of the conquest."[1]

The first Klan — the real Klan — that terrified and lynched and murdered Southern blacks and Southern whites was an agency of the Federal government. It was called the Union League, and like the Klan, it still exists today. The Ku Klux Klan came into existence as a result of, and as a reaction to, the illegal, unconstitutional and criminal activities of the Union League.

Among these activities was the creation of a huge all black force, led by white officers, in the former Confederacy and were funded by clandestine and unconstitutional means. This force was composed of at least 200,000 ex-slaves and former black Union troops. This militia was to be used as the private armies of the carpetbagger governors in all the Southern states. In addition to insuring that voting by terror kept them in power, these militia forces defended against other ambitious carpetbaggers who attempted to usurp illegal power with illegal force.

The white leadership of the Union League directed this enormous black army to terrorise, torture, and kill "reactionary" blacks who would not go along with the new social agenda of the Radical Republicans, including those who would not vote for them.

This same Union League militia conducted a reign of terror against Southern whites, including widespread torture, arson, and murders, to prevent them from assuming their rightful status as citizens.

The long-term consequences of the Union League's activities have been much more significant and dangerous than the Klan's because of its attachment to the Federal government. The Union League's actions were a vital part of national policy programs to eradicate racism and the spirit of rebellion. The paradox is that it has exacerbated racial antagonism and hatred of federal authority.

The story of the Union League is not just an historical episode but relates to contemporary America. It helped generate a body of national laws which set legal precedents for federal race relations policy *today*. As a result, Washington treats many Americans now as if they were racist, reactionary traitors, just as if Reconstruction still existed in every state of the Union.

Modern historians, if they mention the Union League and its militia at all, tend to escribe its undertakings as little more than a series of playful pranks committed by a troupe of benevolent comics. This is no doubt because its role does not conform to the contemporary sanitised and politically correct view of our past.[2]

---

[1] Jessie Pearl Rice, *J.L.M. Curry: Southerner, Statesman and Educator* (New York: Kings Crown Press, 1949), p. 55.

[2] Otis Singletary, *Negro Militia and Reconstruction* (Austin: The University of Texas Press, 1957), p. 5.

THE U.S. SANITARY COMMISSION:

FORERUNNER OF THE UNION LEAGUE

THE CREATION OF THE UNION LEAGUE is a circuitous story and begins during the War Between the States. In April 1861, after the capture of Fort Sumter, President Lincoln called for 75,000 volunteers to join the Union Army. The war began to move into high gear. This call to arms galvanised the spirit of private philanthropy that permeated American culture at that time. Charities of every description were enlisted in the service of the war effort. Women's aid groups were at the center of this movement.

Reverend Dr. Henry Whitney Bellows was the minister at All Souls Unitarian Church in New York. He had a great desire to help the soldiers, but realised that without a clear common goal these women's groups would diffuse their enthusiasm. Dr. Bellows was a prime force behind the "Women's Central Association of Relief," a union of church, social, and fraternal societies devoted to this aid. It was designed to minimise the rivalries and friction between the groups.

Dr. Bellows went to Washington, D.C., to convince the Army's Medical Bureau to allow the Central Association to improve sanitary conditions among the soldiers, since more troops died of disease than were killed in combat: They were transported in open cattle cars in winter; their blankets and clothing were shoddy. They slept in open tents, often on the ground; and their food was unwholesome.

On the train ride down to Washington, Bellows developed the idea of a "Sanitary Commission," to supersede the Central Association, to implement this role. Yet, when he spoke to President Lincoln and his cabinet about the Sanitary Commission, he was initially rebuffed. Lincoln felt it would be as useful as a "fifth wheel on a coach,"[3] but Dr. Clement Furley, the head of the Medical Bureau, did approve. He believed that Lincoln's call for volunteers was futile, since they would never make good soldiers. Furley accepted the Sanitary Commission as long as it restricted its help to the volunteers, but Bellows saw the Sanitary Commission becoming a "great government department."[4] And it did; expanding far beyond the strict constraints that the Army had placed on it. Eventually it evolved into the contemporary American Red Cross.

During the war the Sanitary Commission sent agents and medicine to 500 battles. It coordinated the efforts of 7,000 aid societies and drew its supplies from them. It set up lodges where exhausted or convalescing soldiers could find a meal and a night's rest. It placed feeding stations on the route from the battlefield to the hospital, helped the veteran get his back pay, and kept the wounded soldier in touch with his family. The Sanitary Commission distributed among army surgeons monographs on recent advances in medicine, naively believing that superb surgical articles would stimulate the minds of doctors who were knee-deep in blood, amputated parts, and frenzy.[5]

[3] William Quentin Maxwell, *Lincoln's Fifth Wheel: The Political History of the United States Sanitary Commission* (New York: Longmans, Green and Co., 1956), p. 8.

[4] *Ibid.*, p. 9.

[5] *Ibid.*, p. 42.

THE U.S. SANITARY COMMISSION:

FROM AID TO POLITICS

FROM DR. BELLOW'S PERSPECTIVE, only men of the highest intelligence could understand the Commission's mission. He arrogantly believed that the Commission's "scientific basis" and its "profound regard for politico-economic principles" were the true basis from which "human work must proceed."[6] One of these superior beings was Frederick Law Olmsted. Bellows picked him to be the Secretary-General, the key administrative role. Olmsted was a great executive. He was also a political fanatic and rabidly anti-Southern.

Olmsted was a short, slight man with a limp. In his late 30s, he was already internationally famous in two completely different areas. He first gained notoriety in the 1850s as a writer, with accounts of his travels in the South. He painted a vivid, although biased, picture of its slave-holding society. *A Journey in the Seaboard Slave States* (1857), *A Journey in the Back Country* (1860), and *Journeys and Explorations in the Cotton Kingdom* (1861). All of his books demanded the abolition of slavery.[7]

In addition, Olmsted was a renowned landscape architect. He planned and executed Central Park in New York City, Prospect Park in Brooklyn, South Park in Chicago, and Mt. Royal Park in Montreal.

Olmsted had shown great managerial skill in the Central Park project by superintending 15,000 workers.

More than for public beauty, these large parks had an underlying metaphoric truth for Olmsted. They advanced human morality and happiness by depending on government control since they were "formulated on the philosophical base for the creation of state and national parks."[8]

Because of Olmsted's vision, the Sanitary Commission's mission of mercy gave birth to the political activist offshoot which would become the Union League. Olmsted saw the idea of a Union League as a tool to fight the political heresies that bedeviled the Union cause during the war. He viewed the guiding principal of the Constitution (state sovereignty, the doctrine of decentralised power, and a limited role for the federal government) as a negative and destructive force which made it more difficult to win the war against the Confederates. Olmsted detested the fact that Washington allowed each state to raise its own troops. This made national discipline hard to achieve.

State sovereignty also thwarted the plans of the Sanitary Commission, whose success depended upon the obliteration of local power. The national government, as super-eminent above the states, was the animating principle of the Commission.[9]Bellows and Olmsted believed that state and local benevolent aid work "were mere trifles, ephemeral and inconsistent efforts without method or philosophy."[10]

In August 1862, the Democratic Party, which was opposed to the war, won startling victories in New York, Pennsylvania, Ohio,

Indiana, Illinois and Wisconsin. Soon secret anti-war and anti-Lincoln administration societies began to emerge: The Knights of the Golden Circle, The Sons of Liberty, *etc.*

This dissent was due to the way that the Republicans had pursued the conduct of the war. To protect loyal states from "internal enemies," the Federal government imprisoned those who, they claimed, helped the rebellion by speech or the written word. Democrats played on the danger of tyranny and the loss of liberty. Olmsted and Bellows felt this threatened to rend the national fabric.

The Democratic gubernatorial winner in New York State was Horatio Seymour. He was a dedicated believer in state sovereignty. He defied Abraham Lincoln's call for a military draft quota. Seymour called conscription unconstitutional and refused to comply with the quota for the state until he was threatened with an invasion by Federal troops.

New York's Democratic mayor, Fernando Wood, echoed Seymour's views when he tried to legally transform New York into a "free city," independent of national or state governmental authority. When Horatio Seymour became governor, Bellows and Olmsted believed that Northern divisiveness might clear the way for a Confederate victory.

Olmsted wrote that the times called for an examination of attitude. Middle class respectability was setting its teeth "in the old revolutionary way." It would stamp out treason, even if the war "took seven years" and the citizens put up a "gallows in every town."[11]

For Olmsted and Bellows, the politics of Seymour and Wood urgently demanded that the ideals of the Sanitary Commission should be promoted through a national club. They sent out a letter to prominent New Yorkers to explore the possibility of interest in such an organisation, to be called the "Union League." This club would further the cause for a strong, centralised government to promote unity, and the loyalty to win the war. Many of the replies demonstrate that New Yorkers saw the flaw in their thinking. For instance: "Mr B. [a distinguished lawyer] objects somewhat to your 'objects,' though approving the general design '[t]o oppose state rights dogmas open or insidious,' he thinks is wrong, because it is certain that states, as such, have certain rights that ought to be upheld."[12]

Yet Bellows did not understand. He wrote: "The doctrine of State Sovereignty carried to the point of denying the constitutional right of the nation and the government to protect and preserve the Union at all hazards, was still maintained by politicians in the North. A suicidal doubt infected one considerable party in the country, [the Democrats] as to the possibility of holding the states in open rebellion against their free will ... the party in the North most accustomed to rely on Southern votes [Democrats] gave a dangerous support to the rebellion by discountenancing all energy in the government in its efforts to quench the fires of secession ... [Union men] feared that civil war would break out in the North, when rebellion was raging in the South."[13]

In January 1863 the Union League became a reality after Bellows attended a dinner at the Willard Hotel in Washington. He heard Secretary of State Seward make a speech, in which he said that loyal men had to put the country ahead of the Constitution, because a nation on fire made any debate on the sanctity of law out of order.

Bellows embodied Seward's ideas in his sermon, *Unconditional Loyalty*. Olmsted called it a great work and 30,000 copies were distributed to the Army through the Sanitary Commission. *Unconditional Loyalty* exalted politics, making it an honour to those who had abandoned it in disgust. Bellows said the citizens should concentrate all thoughts, feelings and "views on national subjects" into a club. This club became the Union League.

The New York Union League was the first to see the light of day. It would soon be the most powerful, with 30 branches in that state. Then Boston, Philadelphia and every major city and town had a League club. Later, Secretary of State Seward said that the Union League did much to save the United States from insurrection by restoring confidence and doubling resolution.

Neither Bellows nor Olmsted were deep political thinkers. They did not understand the consequences of the League's activism, but others did. Mrs. Elizabeth Hamilton Schuyler, the great granddaughter of Alexander Hamilton, was critical of Olmsted's political principles and his love of centralised power. She pointed out that he was not alone in this, for many young men thought as he did: "All tend now toward centralisation, unconstitutional and illegal, or despotic measures...a revolution at home, and a dictator."[14]

[6] *Ibid.*, p. 6.

[7] Frederick Law Olmsted, *A Journey in The Seaboard Slave States In The Years 1853-1854, With Remarks On Their Economy* (New York: G. Putnam's Sons, 1904); *A Journey In The Back Country In The Winter of 1853-1854* (New York: Mason Brothers, 1860) *and Journeys And Explorations in the Cotton Kingdom. A Traveler's Observations on Cotton and Slavery in the American Slave States* (London: S. Low, 1861).

[8] *Landscape and Architecture*, Vol. XLIII, No. 1, pp. 12-13.

[9] Henry Whitney Bellows, Historical *Sketch of the Union League Club of New York 1863-1879* (New York: Union League Club, 1879), p. 6.

[10] Maxwell, p. 9.

[11] *Ibid.*, p. 197.

[12] Bellows, p. 23.

[13] *Ibid.*, p. 33.

[14] Maxwell, p. 339.

THE UNION LEAGUE AND

RECONSTRUCTION

SINCE THE BASIC TENETS of the Union League for a strong, centralised state, paralleled the policies of the Republican Party, it is logical that most of its national officers were Federal Republican employees.

Judge James Edmunds was national Union League President from 1863 to 1869. Simultaneously he was the Republican Commissioner of the General Land Office in Washington — a very lucrative office. Through his efforts the National Council of the League joined forces with Republican leaders to combine their resources for a Southern organising campaign to bring loyalty and nationalised patriotism to the "traitorous South." This process fused the League to the Republican Party.

Edmunds said: "For a full year before any plan of restoration had been adopted by Congress [March 1867] the League was actually pushed into the South, for a double purpose of resisting rebel outrages, and of laying the foundation for a truly Republican policy."[15]

Even in the North, the League followed the same tactics as the Republican carpetbaggers in the South. The League cried "fraud" against "the majority on the side of anarchy," when Democrats won

10

again in New York in 1868. The League sought an investigation to change the vote count.[16]

As the Republican Party's Southern arm, the League controlled nominations for office, influenced policy, and functioned as a Radical machine within the Republican Party following the vengeful policies of Thaddeus Stevens, Ben Wade, *etc.*

Then the 15th Amendment to the Constitution gave blacks voting rights while disenfranchising many Southern whites. The League evangelised among the enfranchised freedmen. Paid organisers traveled through the South, initiating blacks into the League, which established a tradition of black Republican voting that lasted for decades.

In every black district there was a League council. In each state these councils were held together by a grand council. The grand councils were, in turn, centralised in a national grand council with headquarters in New York City.

The Union League's political role in the South has always been unclear because of its secrecy. This was a powerful element in making it irresistible to the freed blacks. To become Republican voters, they had to undergo a clandestine initiation ceremony. It was held at night and skillfully devised to heighten the effect.

In a school room or a church, after a torchlight speech by a white League leader, the freedmen declared their loyalty to the Union and sang the national anthem. Then they underwent a final ritual. The "fire of liberty" was lit on the altar. Then the candidates placed their hands upon the flag and took the oath of allegiance to the United States. Then, "right hand to Heaven, thumb and third finger touching their ends over palms, say 'Liberty.' Hand to shoulder, say 'Lincoln.' Hand to side, say 'Loyal.' Hand and finger on chests, other thumb in waistband, say 'League.'"[17]

---

[15] Michael Fitzgerald, The *Union League Movement in the Deep South* (Baton Rouge: Louisiana State University Press, 1989), p. 12.

[16] Bellows, p. 11.

[17] J.G. deRoulhac Hamilton, "The Union League in North Carolina," *Sewanee Review*, Vol. 20 (1912), p. 491.

THE FREEDMEN'S BUREAU ABSORBS

UNION LEAGUE

EVEN THOUGH THE UNION LEAGUE was the Southern arm of the Republican Party, the former Confederate states were still under military occupation. civil law scarcely existed. The Army was the only real government in the "late states in rebellion." Voting was manipulated by the military. It was the true power behind the puppet carpetbag administrations. Thus, inescapably, the Union League's political and vote building activities were absorbed into the military's political and social policy agency: The Freedmen's Bureau.

Supposedly the Bureau had been created to help the former slaves make the difficult transition to citizenship. Hundreds of thousands of them wandered around the South without the job skills or education to survive on their own. The Freedmen's Bureau was to supply them with these tools. Yet this noble idea had a different reality. Since the Bureau was an arm of the War Department, its activities took on the colouration of the Army's basic objective: to turn the former Confederacy into a colony of the victorious North.

Its full title, "The Bureau of Freedmen, Abandoned Lands and Refugees," shows the full extent of its power and jurisdiction. It controlled four million ex-slaves and millions of whites (the "refugees" displaced by the war) and the tens of millions of acres of property that were confiscated from the "traitors."

The Commissioner of the Freedmen's Bureau was Oliver Otis Howard. General Howard's right arm had been blown off at the Battle of Seven Pines. This severe wound embittered him against the South. Here Howard describes his agency's enormous despotic power:

> The law establishing the Bureau committed it to "the control of all subjects relating to the refugees and freedmen from rebel states ... and this almost unlimited authority gave me scope and liberty of action ... legislative, judicial and executive powers were combined in my commission ... [I controlled] all abandoned land solely for the purpose of assigning, leasing and selling them to refugees and freedmen[18]

This meant that General Howard was an absolute dictator and the Freedmen's Bureau was a shadow government, being backed by the armed forces.

President Andrew Johnson pointed out the consequences of the Freedmen's Bureau's having unlimited "scope of action" against civilians, without any restraints:

> The power thus given to the commanding officer over all the people ... is that of an absolute monarch. He alone is permitted to determine what rights of persons and property ... it places at his disposal all the lands and goods in his district and he may distribute them without let or hindrance to whom he pleases. Being bound by no state law, and there being no other law to regulate the subject, he may make a criminal code of his own, and he can make it as bloody as any recorded in history ... Everything is a crime which he chooses to call so and persons are condemned who he pronounces to be guilty ... he may

14

arrest his victims wherever he finds them, without warrant, accusation or proof of probable cause.[19]

MILITARY TRIBUNALS FOR CIVILIANS

The Freedmen's Bureau had its own military court system, which overruled or replaced all local civil courts. This meant that private citizens were tried under military justice: guilty until proven innocent, no writ of habeas corpus, no jury, no required records of proceedings, verdicts rendered in minutes, and sentences (including executions) carried out immediately, often with no trace of the victim's whereabouts or remains ever to be known or found.

MASS CONFISCATION

The Freedmen's Bureau also unconstitutionally confiscated millions of acres of private property. Bureau military courts loosely interpreted the wartime Confiscation Acts to expropriate massive tracts of choice plantations for private gain. Much of this confiscation was publicly rationalised in the name of redistribution for the blacks and to "re-educate" the former "traitors." Large property holdings were associated with the classic Southern aristocratic class, with cotton plantations and their slaves. Eventually "nearly two million of the farms had been given away by the government."[20]

RELOCATION AS RE-EDUCATION

The Freedmen's Bureau was responsible for defusing the threat of another war by repopulating the South with loyal Northerners on that confiscated land. It then forcibly moved these displaced Southerners into the North temporarily to change them mentally away from being "rebels" to transform them into loyal and "progressive" Unionists.

General John Eaton, one of the creators of the Freedmen's Bureau, said:

> The educational influence of the change was noticeable and most important ... returning to the South, after perhaps a year's absence, to the neighbourhood of their former homes ... [the] transformation through living in the midst of the industries of the North, was very great. They had made the discovery that the possession of a vast property and the ownership of slaves ... was not essential to self-respect or social standing.[21]

EDUCATION FOR RE-EDUCATION

The Freedmen's Bureau also had the first peacetime federal educational mandate. Overtly, it was to teach the ex-slaves so that they could survive as free men. Covertly, this education was to transform whites, at the same time, into "good" citizens.

J.P. Wickersham, a noted Radical Republican, stated this clearly:

> What can education do for the non-slave holding whites of the South? The great majority are deplorably ignorant ... As long as they are ignorant they will remain tools of political demagogues and therefore be incapable of self-government. They must be educated ... A republican form of government cannot last long without providing a system of free schools ...

16

Ignorant voters endanger liberty. With free schools in the South there will be no rebellion in the future ... when our youth learn to read similar books, similar lessons, we will become one person, possessing one organic nationality.[22]

Then Congress forced a federalised education into the South through new state constitutions which compelled tax-supported schools controlled by Washington. The Freedmen's Bureau set this nationalising process in motion. First, a portion of the Southern property confiscated by the Bureau was converted into schools. "2,118 schools [are] under the care of the Bureau."[23]

Congress mandated that the Bureau should have an educational arm, but initially it authorised no funds for this role. So the Bureau financed its own schools without Congressional approval or citizen acceptance. The method for doing so set the precedent for the modern illegal, off-budget funding methods. The expenses of the schools were met with the proceeds of rents, sale of crops, school taxes and tuition, and sale of "Confederate States" property. The amount raised from all these miscellaneous sources was $1,865,645.40."[24] By today's standards, this is more like 1.8 billion dollars.

THE UNION LEAGUE, AGENCY OF THE FREEDMEN'S BUREAU

The Union League fused with the Freedmen's Bureau as a result of the Congressional Reconstruction. Before 1867 Bureau officials had been actively at work among the freedmen, with the view of using them politically for the Republican Party. Simultaneously, Bureau men had done all in their power to alienate the Southern blacks from the Southern whites.

After the freedmen were enfranchised (1867), it was apparent that there was a great necessity to control them in the interest of the carpetbaggers and national policy. Another organisation was needed to appeal to the freedmen's pride and their emotions as it organised them.

The Union League furnished the ideal instrument *via* its mysterious and emotional rituals. Thus it won the undying hatred of the Southern whites; the very name of "Union League" has remained the symbol of all that was evil in Reconstruction.[25]

---

[18] Annual Report of the Secretary of War, for the year 1869, p. 499. All annual reports in this article were published by the Government Printing Office.

[19] *The Congressional Globe*, 39th Congress, 1st Session (Washington, D.C.: Reprint Edition by United States Historical Documents Institute, Inc., 1970), p. 463.

[20] Annual Report of the Secretary of Agriculture, for the year 1896, p. xlvi.

[21] John Eaton, Grant, *Lincoln and the Freedmen* (New York: St. Martin's Press, 1903), p. 37.

[22] J.P. Wickersham, Education *as an Element in the Reconstruction of the Union* (Boston: G.C. Rand and Avery, 1865), p. 2.

[23] Annual Report of the Secretary of War, for the year 1869, p. 506.

[24] *Ibid.*, pp. 506 and 509

[25] Hamilton, p. 486.

THE UNION LEAGUE: FREEDMEN'S

BUREAU'S MILITIA

WITHIN TWO YEARS after the end of the War, the Secretary of War declared that only 48,081 men were left in the armed services.[26] With peace, the military had become very cost-conscious. Yet a large force was required to occupy the defeated Southern states. So militia forces were raised in each former Confederate state. Their expenses were covered without Federal taxes, the same way that schools were paid for: confiscation. For example,

> It was made the duty of the Governor [of Alabama] by an ordinance ... to organise immediately 137 companies of volunteer militia ... all proceeds of the sale of contraband and captured property seized or captured by the militia will constitute a part of the fund out of which they will be paid, thus inciting the volunteers to harass the people in time of peace by unlawful seizure to provide the means of paying themselves.[27]

These militia forces would soon consist entirely of black troops who were all members of the Union League, and would participate in full-scale battles.

The Federal Constitution authorises that each state maintain a militia. For the post-war South this would mean re-arming the former Confederates. This was unacceptable to Washington.

The Radicals were able to abolish the provisional militia [the white militia] with comparative ease. On 2 March 1867, the same day that the first Reconstruction Act was passed, an obscure rider to the annual Appropriation Act for the Army ordered the disbandment of all militia forces in the Southern states and prohibited the "further organisation, arming or calling into service of the said militia, or any part thereof," until so authorised by Congress.[28]

President Andrew Johnson protested that this was unconstitutional, but to no avail.

Once disbanded, the white militia was replaced by an all-black militia, mostly consisting of Union Army veterans. This new militia took on a sinister Radical perspective. It grew out of the stern dictates of the Union League and Freedmen's Bureau plan for a permanent Republican South. The militia forces were assigned to the task of perpetuating the existence of the newly created Republican carpetbag state governments. In reality this meant the creation of private armies controlled by the governors of each conquered state. It was alleged that they were to quell Southern violence, but, more accurately, they were to subdue Republican carpetbag political rivals.[29]

Arming the black militia, which usually had white carpetbagger officers, was bitterly opposed by Conservatives. This led to the carpetbag governors "borrowing" guns and ammunition from Northern armouries. This was inadequate because there were as many as some quarter-million black militia men under arms in the South. Then the governors turned to the federal government for aid.[30]

First, Governor William Holden of North Carolina sent his political associate, William G. Clarke, to Washington. He met with Ulysses S. Grant and Montgomery Meigs, the Quartermaster-General of the Army. Grant agreed to outfit the North Carolina black militia.[31]

Soon after the organisation of the Union League in North Carolina, in 1867, arms were procured and many local League councils were converted into military companies which were drilled constantly. They became a menace to the peace. They drilled on the open roads. Armed sentinels were posted on both sides of the roads to turn back anyone who might come up.[32]

Congress then passed a law authorising the distribution of Federal arms to Southern states on a quota basis.[33]

In the 1868 Presidential election, Grant was victorious in those Southern states in relation to their military preparedness. In Tennessee, Florida, North Carolina, South Carolina, and Arkansas, where the militia was organised before the election, Grant won. In Louisiana and Georgia, where no militia was organised by November 1868, Horatio Seymour won.[34]

Each governor was commander-in-chief of the militia. He could call it out whenever he deemed that the circumstances warranted it. The governor was empowered to assess and collect taxes from rebellious counties to defray the cost of militia operations there. His grip on the militia was assured because he had complete control of the selection of officers.[35]

22

[26] Annual Report of the Secretary of War, for the year 1868, p.

[27] *The Congressional Globe*, 40th Congress, 2nd Session, p. 510.

[28] *The Congressional Globe*, 39th Congress, 2nd Session, p. 217.

[29] Singletary, p. 4.

[30] It is difficult to determine accurately how many Union League militia were under arms. Statistics by state are vague, possibly deliberately so. Governor Holden of North Carolina stated he had 80,000 militiamen. Governor Scott of South Carolina admitted he had 20,000. By taking Scott's lower number and multiplying it by 10 (for the 10 of 11 Southern states under occupation and then adding in Holden's 80,000) we arrive at 280,000 militia. Delaware and Maryland are not counted. They were also under militia occupation, but were Union States.

Also, Proceedings *of the Tax-Payers Convention of South Carolina,* 1874 (Charleston: News and Courier, 1874), p. 95.

[31] Ulysses S. Grant, letter to William T. Sherman, 17 June 1870. W.W. Holden Papers. (Raleigh, North Carolina Department of Archives and History).

[32] *North Carolina Sentinel,* 19 August 1865.

[33] *The Congressional Globe,* 42nd Congress, 3rd Session, p. 300.

[34] Singletary, p. 36.

[35] *Ibid.,* p. 20.

THE UNION LEAGUE MILITIA: PRIVATE

POLITICAL ARMIES

GOVERNOR HOLDEN OF NORTH CAROLINA showed the magnitude of the Union League militia: "I can control at my word, 80,000 men." Holden was head of the Union League in his state, even while governor. Holden told this to a Reverend Smith. Smith replied: "This is a dangerous power. Very dangerous power in the hands of one man." Smith said that Holden answered, that for his own part, in his opinion, General Grant would hold the government of the United States no matter what the election in 1872; that he [Grant] desired him [Holden] to be emperor and his son to succeed him as emperor.[36]

In South Carolina, Governor Scott armed 20,000 black militia men before his re-election in 1870.[37] Thus, in these two states, the League formed a 100,000-man force.

In Alabama, in 1868, the *Columbus Enquirer* gave a report of the League's strength in various towns in an area only 50 miles across, not the whole state.

On Sunday, they met at Mrs. Comer's place, below Hatchechubbe, well-armed, numbering about 600. There is another large League at Spring Hill, numbering 300; another at Enon, numbering 400; another in the neighbourhood of Silver Run, numbering 500; another at Union Springs, numbering 800;

24

and one near Eufala, numbering 1,000. They are thoroughly armed and equipped.[38]

This means that 3,600 Union League militia was operating in one small section of the state.

---

[36] Stanley Horn, The *Invisible Empire*: The Story of the *Ku Klux Klan*, 1866-1871 (Cos Cob, CT.: John E. Edwards, 1969), p. 17.

[37] Francis B. Siskins and R.H. Woody, *South Carolina during Reconstruction* (Chapel Hill: The University of North Carolina Press, 1932), p. 451.

[38] *Mobile Register*, 14 October 1868.

CARPETBAGGERS MAKE WAR ON

CARPETBAGGERS

REPUBLICAN GOVERNORS used their Union League militias to prevent their Republican rivals from taking political power by force.

ARKANSAS

The black Union League militia was used most often in Arkansas. This produced the famous "Brooks-Baxter War." In the 1872 gubernatorial election, Republicans split into Liberal and Radical factions. The Liberals rallied to evangelist Joseph Brooks, former chaplain of a United States Army coloured regiment. The Radicals chose Elisha Baxter, a circuit judge. His qualifications: indicted for treason by the Confederacy.

There were many irregularities in the voting. Baxter was declared the winner. Brooks attempted an injunction from the courts, but his case was dismissed. Later, a second appeal favoured Brooks. Armed with a court order and the militia, Brooks forced Baxter out of the Statehouse. Baxter set up his government at Anthony House, also in Little Rock. President Grant refused to recognise either man. Baxter declared martial law and called up his own militia. Both sides broke into arsenals for weapons. Reinforcements poured into Little Rock for both sides. There was much firing. Grant telegraphed both sides to disband. Neither did. There was more fighting. Then Grant recognised Baxter. The war was over.[39]

LOUISIANA

In no other state was the militia so exclusively the governor's private army. In 1868 Henry Clay Warmoth, a former Union Army officer, was elected Republican governor. In 1870 the Republican Party split into Radical and Liberal factions. In August 1871 Warmoth and Lt. Governor P.B.S. Pinchback, a black, successfully bid for re-election, although a second term was illegal. They were opposed by the "Custom House" faction; S.B. Packard, a U.S. Marshal, and George Carter, Speaker of the Louisiana House of Representatives.

January 1872: The legislature convened. Carter was expelled. A Warmoth man was installed as speaker. Carter's supporters set up a second legislature over the Gem Saloon on Royal Street in New Orleans, protected by deputised citizens. Warmoth called up 5,000 militia, headed by former Confederate general, James Longstreet. They forcibly took possession of the Gem Saloon building. Carter's legislators then met at the Cosmopolitan Club and counter-attacked the Statehouse. They failed. A second attack was aborted when President Grant ordered U.S. troops against Carter. His men returned to Warmoth's Statehouse.[40]

October - November 1872: Five different slates of candidates. Warmoth broke with President Grant, had a fusion ticket with Liberal Republicans and the hated Democrats. He was opposed by Packard and John McEnery. Election Day. Two returning boards, two winners. Packard seized Mechanics Institute for his Statehouse.

Legislators impeached Warmoth and Kellogg was declared the winner. Warmoth occupied Lyceum Hall. Again, two legislatures, two governors: Kellogg and McEnery. Lt. Governor Pinchback, still in office, called in the militia against Warmoth. McEnery called his militia and attacked the police station. He was repulsed. His legislators were arrested. There were still two governors.

1874: Kellogg and McEnery used their militia to fight a pitched battle with artillery and Gatling guns. Kellogg's militia surrendered. Now, one governor: McEnery. President Grant ordered in Federal troops. Kellogg was put into the Statehouse.

1876: Gubernatorial election. Again, two governors. Both Packard and Conservative Francis Nichols claimed victory. Packard, the Republican, seized the Statehouse. Then Rutherford B. Hayes was elected President. In April 1877 he ordered all Federal troops withdrawn from the South. Packard quickly left for England, as U.S. consul.[41]

MISSISSIPPI:

November 1870: James L. Alcorn, a Conservative Republican, was elected governor. In November 1871 Alcorn resigned, to succeed Hiram Revels as a United States senator. By 1873 Alcorn once again entered the Mississippi gubernatorial race. His opponent was carpetbagger Adelbert Ames, the other Mississippi senator. Ames won.

Ames was a Radical Republican, and a former Union Army officer. In 1868 he was a provisional governor, a military governor, until Alcorn was elected. Under Ames's rule, black office holders increased and the Union League militia increased and so did violence. He was hated by the local whites. Ames said that since the "state government commands respect of the coloured race only, it must depend for military support on coloured troops."[42]

In addition to the League militia, Governor Ames attempted to create a metropolitan police force, which meant another personal army loyal to him. This failed, but he succeeded in passing legislation disbanding existing, competing militias, and confiscating their arms for his own forces.[43]

In 1870 Ames resigned from the Army and through false credentials, was seated in the U.S. Senate. There he worked for black dominance in the South.

1875 elections: Alcorn tried again, still allied with the Conservative Republicans. During the campaign Alcorn denounced Radical sheriff Brown as a "defaulter" and planned to attend Brown's rebuttal speech. Sheriff Brown assembled the League militia to "protect his right to speak," but in reality, to frighten Alcorn. This provoked a battle of militias, which took place at Friar's Point, Alcorn's home. Women and children were evacuated from the town.

A third militia company was sent to Alcorn's aid. When the smoke cleared, Sheriff Brown's militia was in retreat. Governor Ames responded by putting several additional Union League militia companies on a war footing. All sides paraded and menaced each other. It seemed all-out war was imminent.

United States Attorney-General Edwards Pierrepont sent G.K. Chase to negotiate a compromise, a "Peace Agreement." Ames agreed to disband his League militia if the other sides deposited their arms with Federal troops in Jackson, and with the assurance of a peaceful and orderly election.

Without their private armies the carpetbaggers were overwhelmed and the Democrats easily won over the legislature. They planned to impeach Ames but he resigned first.[44]

TEXAS

Governor Edmund Davis used the militia freely during the election of 1871 and martial law in the same period. In December 1873 Davis was defeated by Judge Richard Coke. Davis used his militia to retake the Austin Statehouse. When President Grant refused to send Federal troops, Davis capitulated.[45]

SOUTH CAROLINA

Governor Scott armed his 20,000 black militia men before his election in 1870. Scott said: "I will carry the election here with the militia ... I am giving out ammunition all the time."[46]

A prominent South Carolinian complained that during the election campaign of 1870, almost every public meeting was "attended by the militia of General Scott."[47]

TENNESSEE

Governor Brownlow mobilised the militia just prior to the election in which he defeated Emerson Etheridge. Three years later he took flight from the state.[48]

GEORGIA

Governor Bullock won a fraudulent election as the Union League militia herded the blacks to the polls.[49]

---

[39] Singletary, pp. 51-65.

[40] *Ibid.*, pp. 66-71.

[41] *Ibid.*, pp. 72-80.

[42] James Garner, *Reconstruction In Mississippi* (New York: Macmillan and Co., 1901), p. 385.

[43] Edward Mayes, Lucius *Q. C. Lamar: His Life, Times and Speeches*, 1825-1893 (Nashville: Methodist Episcopal Church South, 1896), p. 239.

[44] Singletary, pp. 81-97.

[45] *New York Herald*, 17, 18 January 1874.

[46] *Report of Joint Investigating Committee On Public Frauds, General Assembly of South Carolina, 1877-1878* (Columbia, 1878), p. 675.

[47] House of Representatives Report No. 22, Vol. II, Part 3, 42nd Congress, 2nd Session, p. 1185.

[48] James W. Patton, *Unionism and Reconstruction in Tennessee*, 1860-1869 (Chapel Hill: The University of North Carolina Press, 1934), p. 176.

[49] Horn, p. 173.

BLACK MILITIA VS. BLACK

DEMOCRATS

SINCE BLACKS WERE THE MAJORITY of voters in many Southern states, it was imperative that they should adhere to the new values and the "new social order" that the carpetbaggers promised. They were compelled to join the League's militia as part of that program. Some refused to join and refused to vote Republican, preferring to be guided by their former master's advice as they entered political life. For the Union League, this was treason; a very dangerous menace to the solidarity of the race. Militia men were ordered to deal with such unruly members of their race in a way that would convince them of the wisdom of yielding to Northern guidance and of embracing the policy of violent hostility toward the whites.

The treatment accorded to the dissenting blacks was usually effective, and a small proportion dared to remain out of accord with the majority of their colour. Those who did were subjected to every type of violence and intimidation.[50]

For instance, in Franklin County, Tennessee, the members of the Union League kept the citizens in a constant state of alarm by marching through the town, night after night, making noisy demonstrations with fife and drum and boisterous shouts and flourishing their weapons. An explosion came when a Conservative black had the temerity to make a political speech. Armed League members broke up the meeting and marched away firing their guns in the air. That night there was a fearful clash between an armed party of Conservatives, black and white, and a parade of exulting League members, who attempted to prevent the Conservatives from demonstrating on the public square. When the gunfire subsided and the smoke cleared away, one white Conservative was dead and six white and six black Conservatives were wounded. Twenty-seven League men were wounded.[51]

Mass meetings of blacks were held quite often in Augusta and Macon, Georgia. At one of them, during the 1868 presidential campaign, this banner was displayed: "Every man [Negro] that don't vote the Radical ticket, this is the way we want to serve him: hang him by the neck." Perhaps nowhere in the state was the persecution of non-Radical blacks more severe than in the country surrounding Macon and the city itself.[52]

In Franklin County, North Carolina, in 1868, the League sent a deputation to attack a reputable white farmer who had given freedmen advice not to join the League.[53] In Wilmington, North Carolina, a black man was severely whipped by order of the League.[54]

In other towns there were similar cases. Instances of this sort might be multiplied indefinitely, for they occurred all over the state. Notices containing threats were posted. This example was placed on the door of a Conservative black in Hillsboro, North Carolina.

Notice for Thomas Green. A damn Concurvitive we understand you were out with Concurvitive Lys, but d-n your time if you don't look out you will catch h-l surely. We herd you come very near catching it in Sharlot and if you don't mind you will catch it in Hills Boro shure enough and that right. If you d-n Concurvitive friends can protect you, you had better stick near them in that hour for great will be your Deserney. This is the least of our examples. The next time will tell you your will on good behavior. Postscript. You mind me of the sun of Esaw and who sold his birthright for one mossel of meat and so now you have sold your wife and children and yourself for a drink of liquers and have come to be a Concurvitive boot licker. Tom, I would not give a damn for your back in a few days; you Concurvitive....[55]

Daniel Goodloe was the U.S. Marshal for the state of North Carolina for a period of 3 ½ years after the war. He said:

I have also heard of combinations of blacks calling themselves Ku Klux and committing outrages ... It has been charged that they have mobbed blacks for voting the Conservative ticket. In fact, I believe there are well-authenticated cases of the sort.[56]

In Mississippi, in 1870, the state legislature passed an anti-Ku Klux Klan law. It offered a $500 reward for conviction of any person found guilty of violent crime in disguise. The first claim for this reward and first indictment under this act grew out of a Ku Kluxing of a Democratic black named Adam Kennard, by a group of hostile blacks in Ku Klux disguise, led by a notorious white Radical. From this incident came the famous Meridian riot of June 1871.

In March 1871, Kennard, as Deputy Sheriff, attempted to arrest three blacks for breaking their labour contracts. One night, disguised men whipped, shot and wounded Kennard. The assault was by blacks, who were led by a Scallywag, Daniel Price. Kennard had Price and the blacks arrested under the new anti-Klan law. Price was a fanatic Radical and a long-time criminal. Price advised the blacks in Livingston to arm and burn the town to ashes. Price was the superintendent of schools in Meridian. His trial was in Livingston.

Kennard had many armed white supporters at the trial. Price threatened to bring in his armed black followers into court. Price was allowed to forfeit bond and sneak away to avoid mass bloodshed. Price's black friends were outraged at his secret getaway.

A week later the blacks met in the courthouse. Then they had a noisy, threatening march in the street. When a storehouse was set on fire, the whites came out to stop it. The blacks refused to help. One white Radical shouted: "Yes. Kill all their women and children, too!"

The ringleaders were arrested. At the arraignment there was a fight between a witness and a defendant. One defendant, Tyler, shot the judge in the head. Pistol fire exploded in the courtroom. In minutes, 300 armed men were in the streets of Meridian. Several defendants were killed.[57]

---

[50] Hamilton, p. 487.

[51] Horn, p. 75.

[52] Roberta F. Cason, "The Union League in Georgia" *Georgia Historical Quarterly*, Vol. 20 (1936), p. 137.

[53] *North Carolina Sentinel*, 21 August 1868.

[54] *Ibid.*, 20 July 1868.

[55] Hamilton, p. 487.

[56] Thomas F. Bayard, "Ku Klux Klan Organization," speech in United States Senate, 20 March 1871 (Washington: Congressional Globe Printing Office, 1871) p. 6.

[57] Horn, p. 156.

THE UNION LEAGUE BLACK MILITIA

TERRORISES WHITES

THE THIRD FUNCTION of the Union League militia was to control the Southern white population. In South Carolina, white militia leaders seemed to feel an irresistible compulsion to deliver inflammatory speeches to their troops. Joe Crew, a Union League militia captain in Laurens, was quoted as telling his men that if they wanted provisions and could not afford them, they should go into the fields and take what they wanted. If whites did not settle with them the way they thought was right, they should burn them out of house and home. Matches were cheap.[58]

Senator Francis Blair of Missouri said:

The state government [of South Carolina] has not afforded adequate protection to persons and property. In fact, until a late period, by the free exercise of the pardoning power and by the arming of the coloured militia, while the whites were disarmed, gross errors were committed ... We refer to the occurrence which took place at Union. The coloured militia was on a parade, with arms in their hands. They met on the public road a one-armed white man, who had formerly been in the Confederate service, who had some whiskey in his wagon. This they demanded, flourishing their arms. He gave them some. Then they demanded more. This he declined, upon the ground that it was not his property, but belonged to other parties. They deliberately took him from his wagon, carried him into the woods, and there shot him in cold blood with the State arms in their hands.

Here was a flagrant and wanton case of highway robbery and murder, committed under the circumstances as monstrous as it was without the slightest justification. To permit such a case to go unpunished ... would be equivalent to the granting of a roving commission of theft and blood. Five of those identified as engaged in the deed were arrested and committed to jail. An attempt was made to have them removed to another county. An armed band entered the jail and with their own hands executed the law. They left behind a paper stating as a reason, that the removal of the prisoners to Columbia meant their release without trial or punishment.[59]

NORTH CAROLINA

In this state the most common outrage committed by the League militia against whites was barn burning. The loss of the barn meant complete ruin and starvation to the farmer. It went on in every county. Conclusive evidence shows that the burnings were decided upon at League meetings.

For instance, in Gaston County, there were nine barn burnings in one week.[60] Black offenders were arrested and confessed that the League in that county not only sponsored the burnings but were also actively on orders from the head of the League in Raleigh [Governor Holden].[61]

In Edgecombe County, in two months of 1869, there were burnings of two churches, several cotton gins, a cotton factory, barns, and dwellings. Most were traced to black incendiaries.[62] In November 1869, in Orange County, three barns burned at one time in sight of each other. Some of the burnings were ordered by Governor Holden.[63]

State Senator John W. Stephens, a henchman of Governor Holden, at a Yanceyville Union League meeting, gave a book of matches to all the blacks in attendance with the suggestion that they would be useful in burning the white people's houses and barns. There ensued an orgy of arson: nine barns burned in one night. The Yanceyville Hotel burned, a row of brick houses and tobacco crops of several leading citizens were destroyed. Stephens was later executed by the Ku Klux Klan.[64]

Stephens's death provoked Governor Holden to enact the anti-Klan law of 1870, the "Shofer Bill." Holden could then declare any county in insurrection and under martial law, and he could send in his militia. He did so. One company of the militia was commanded by Colonel George Kirk. He was known as "Bloody" Kirk or "Cut Throat" Kirk. During the War Between the States Kirk led pro-Union guerrillas in the East Tennessee Mountains. He committed many atrocities.

Now, under Holden, Kirk provoked what is known as the "Kirk-Holden War." Kirk marched through Caswell and Alamance counties. They were alleged to be in insurrection. Kirk's "Angels" committed crimes which *the New York World* denounced as "a disgrace to the nineteenth century."[65]

Kirk also made wholesale arrests of suspected Klansmen. When some of them obtained writs of habeas corpus, Kirk defied the state Supreme Court by saying, "These things have played out now."[66]

Witnesses testified that Kirk tied a noose around their necks and hung them for a moment to make confessions that they were Klan members. They refused to confess because they were not. It was Governor Holden who gave the instructions to apprehend and torture these men.[67]

Senator Bayard of Delaware spoke before Congress about the crimes perpetrated by Kirk:

> Here are the facts. Fifty or sixty unarmed men were taken without a writ, without colour of law of any kind, dragged from their homes, kept by [Kirk] ... threatened with death instantly should an attempt be made for their rescue; not only were they to be murdered, as helpless prisoners, but the women and children of the town were to be put to fire and sword. And such conduct as this, Senators, is absolutely justified on the floor of the United States Senate.[68]

ARKANSAS

The Union League militia enforced gubernatorial declarations of martial law. The largest operation, in any state, occurred in Arkansas. On 1 November 1868, two days before the general election, Governor Powell Clayton declared martial law. Then came four months of terrorism and internal civil war. The state was divided into four military districts. The entire population of towns in the path of the militia fled. The militia roamed the country, torturing those they captured. Towns like Warren and Hamburg were gutted.[69] It was written:

> Many of the best citizens have fled for safety ... And many others have been arrested ... several men have been shot ... scarcely a cabin in the county has escaped plunder. This work has been going on for more than two months with almost incredible shamelessness.[70]

Even Governor Clayton felt compelled to attempt to explain and apologise for it: "Some evils have resulted from the occupancy of counties by martial law." When "the prisoner was killed while attempting to escape" became such a familiar phrase in the militia commander's reports, even Governor Clayton expressed a desire for more details.[71]

GEORGIA

The state elections of 1868 were bitterly contested and marked by violence. The "Camilla riot" created a sensation in the North, particularly since it was a direct confrontation between the black militia and whites.

There was a march by 300 heavily armed Union League blacks from Albany to Camilla, with two white Republican candidates at their head. They were N.P. Pierce, candidate for Congress, and Mr. Murphy, candidate for elector and head of the Union League in Albany, Georgia. They came to Camilla to attend a Republican mass meeting.

The sheriff of Camilla was alarmed by the size of the group, and galloped out to meet them. He urged them to disband. They refused. The sheriff rode back and gathered a posse, which met the advancing mob. Both sides opened fire: 8 blacks dead, 25 wounded. Two white posse members killed.

This incident gained much notoriety in the North. The Freedmen's Bureau in Albany sent a much distorted picture to the Northern press. They presented it as a "massacre," in which heartless Southern whites butchered helpless blacks in order to prevent their holding a public meeting. Yet even the committee of investigation under carpetbag governor Bullock found that the trouble was caused by Pierce and Murphy attempting to enter Camilla at the head of a large armed group.[72]

ALABAMA

The Union League militia was "constantly parading the streets with guns on their shoulders. You would pass along the road at any time of day and meet those blacks with guns; you could hear them firing constantly during the day time and night time."[73]

Shots were fired indiscriminately by militia men going to and returning from muster. They frequently visited their spite on their white neighbour's property. Dogs and livestock were favourite targets.

In Gainesville, when some of the white people indignantly protested against such high-handed treatment, the blacks replied that "they had the charter from the government at Washington, right direct, and they had the right to guard, and they intended to do so."[74]

League militia men even intimidated white moderate Republican carpetbaggers like Nicholas Davis, who testified that black Leaguers "forbade me to speak here on this street [in Huntsville]. That would provoke [the League]. They forbade me to speak here in front of the court house."[75]

As one resident later said: "The blacks acted here like an invading army after they had conquered and were going roughshod over everything. They thought they were the big dogs in the ring."[76]

MISSISSIPPI

Peter Crosby was the black sheriff of Vicksburg. He was also the head of a company of League militia. A taxpayer's convention in December 1874 forcibly ejected him from office, for his extortion methods. Then Governor Ames mobilised his militia and put Crosby back in office. Then the mayor of Vicksburg put the city under martial law and mobilised the city's militia against Ames.

On 7 December, the two opposing militias clashed twice. The second battle was at Pemberton Monument. Thirty-eight were killed. Federal troops were sent to Vicksburg. They deposed the newly elected sheriff and replaced him with the hated Crosby.[77]

[58] *Columbia (S. C.) Daily Phoenix*, 7 September 1870.

[59] Francis P. Blair, "Protection of Life in The South," speech in the United States Senate, 3, 4 April 1871 (Washington: F. and J. Rives and George A. Bailey. Reporters and printers of the debates of Congress, 1871), p. 14.

[60] Senate Report No. 1, 42nd Congress, 1st Session, p. 365.

[61] Horn, p. 195.

[62] *Tarboro (NC.) Southerner*, 18 November 1869.

[63] Senate Report No. 1, 42nd Congress, 1st Session, p. 191.

[64] Horn, p. 199.

[65] *Ibid.*, p. 199.

[66] *Ibid.*, p. 199.

[67] Bayard, p. 8.

[68] *Ibid.*, p. 5.

[69] Horn, p. 258.

[70] Thomas Black to Andrew Johnson, 14 January 1869. (Andrew Johnson Papers, Library of Congress, Manuscript Division.)

[71] Horn, pp. 259 and 260.

[72] Report of the Committee of Investigation in *Georgia State Journal*, 1868, pp. 353-356.

[73] Testimony of the Rev. Robert W. Shand, House of Representatives Report No. 22, Vol. II, Part 3, 42nd Congress, 2nd Session, p. 905.

[74] Horn, p. 27.

[75] House of Representatives Report No. 262, 43rd Congress, 2nd Session, p. 905.

[76] Horn, p. 27.

[77] Singletary, pp. 84-85.

THE CONGRESSIONAL KKK

COMMITTEE: LEAGUE OR KLAN?

IN 1870 A CONGRESSIONAL COMMITTEE was formed to investigate a new and frightening secret, disguised, terror organisation that had arisen in the occupied South. It was called the Ku Klux Klan. Supposedly it was violently abusing the newly emancipated blacks and was intending to re-institute slavery.

As a result of this Congressional investigation, harsh new federal "force" laws were created, enabling the President and the federal courts to enforce the civil rights provisions of the 14th Amendment, by usurping power from the state courts. Yet, non-radical committee members found that the Ku Klux Klan arose as an inescapable consequence of the Union League's brutality. The Klan was falsely charged with crimes against blacks, as a method to generate more military and political power for the carpetbag governments or to divert national attention away from their enormously corrupt and criminal activities. Many of the crimes against blacks were committed by Union League men disguised as Klansmen.

The Ku Klux Klan committee interviewed hundreds of witnesses. Their testimony filled 13 volumes. Hearsay and rumours were accepted. Testimony was not restricted by time, and questioning was by party prejudice.

There were 21 members of the committee. Thirteen of them, as was expected, condemned the Klan. The minority report took issue with the majority:

Had there been no wanton oppression in the South, there would have been no Ku Kluxism. Had there been no rule of the tyrannical, corrupt, carpetbagger or Scallywag rule, there would have been no secret organisations. From the oppression and corruption of the one sprang the vice and outrage of the other ... when the testimony before us is analysed ... the carpetbaggers, the Freedmen's Bureau agents and Loyal Leaguers [Union Leaguers] who went into these states, took as the theme of their harangues, the wrongs the blacks had suffered and the right they had to take whatever they pleased of the property they had laboured to acquire for their masters; when, in secret sworn organisations, [the Union Leagues] hatred of the white race was instilled into the minds of these ignorant people by every art and wile that bad men could devise; when the blacks were formed into military organisations and the white people of these states were denied the use of arms; when arson, rape, robbery and murder were things of daily occurrence; when the great masses of the most intelligent whites were disenfranchised and the ballot was put into the hands of the blacks by the government at Washington; when every promise made and every law enacted was broken and disregarded by the Federal authorities whenever it suited their purpose to do so; when even the courts were closed and the Federal officers, who were by Congress absolute rulers and dispensers of what they called justice, ignored, insulted and trampled upon the rights of the ostracised and disenfranchised white men while the officials pandered to the enfranchised blacks on whose vote they relied; in short, when the people saw that they had no rights which were respected, no protection from insults, no security even for their wives and little children, and that what little they had saved from the ravages of war was being confiscated by taxation and rendered valueless by the debts for which men who owned nothing had pledged it, and saw that all their complaints and remonstrances, however honestly and humbly presented to Congress, were either wholly disregarded as evidence of a rebellious and unsubdued spirit, many of them took the law into their own hands and did deeds of violence which we neither justify nor excuse. But all history shows that bad government will make bad citizens; and when the corruption, extortion and villainy of the governments which Congress has set up and maintained over the Southern states are thoroughly understood and made known, as we trust they will be some day, the world will be amazed at the long suffering and endurance of that people.[78]

FALSE CHARGES HIDE CORRUPTION

The following comment by Governor Scott of Tennessee, explains the reason for some of the false allegations of outrages against the Klan:

What then can be the object and design in making false and slanderous statements? We will attempt briefly to explain. In the political and civil confusion that immediately succeeded the close of the war, many acts of malfeasance and peculation in office, and frauds upon the state, were committed by railroad rings, public officers, and government agents. The powers of the government were almost entirely subsidised to the interest of individuals, and large fortunes made by a few at the expense of the public treasury. In many instances, indictments for murder and other high crimes were dismissed without trial, all the agencies and resources of the state government were used to the advantage of the few and to the injury of the many.... Hence the clamour in order to evade or prevent an investigation of their official acts, and to excite sympathy of those abroad who do not know of their misdoings and malversion in office. They wish to make good men in other states believe that they are martyrs to their political faith, and thus excite the sympathy of all lovers of the Union, and cause places of profit to be assigned to them by the President or Congress, after they have lost the confidence and good opinion of a people whom they have outraged and embarrassed by their maladministration.[79]

FALSE CHARGES STRENGTHEN UNION LEAGUE

William H. Smith, the Republican governor of Alabama, wrote this letter in 1870, describing the false outrage charges against the Klan, which bolstered the Union League and the carpetbag governments:

The Republicans are earnest in their efforts to deceive the people in the North in relation to the conditions of the South. Senator Morton, of Indiana, and Spencer, of Alabama, have made speeches in the Senate, alleging that riot, bloodshed, and anarchy reign in Alabama, North Carolina and other Southern states; and that Union men are at the mercy of the "Ku Klux" and dare not speak their sentiments without danger of their lives and property. These speeches are being distributed all over the country by the Radical Executive Committee, in order to deceive the people, and to furnish an excuse for President Grant, who has ordered United States troops to North Carolina to aid Governor Holden.[80]

FALSE KLAN AMBUSH

Riots that occurred during the 1870 campaign and election corroborated reports to President Grant of the unsettled conditions in Alabama caused by the ghostly visitations of the Ku Klux Klan. James S. Perrin, a Union Leaguer and deputy marshal, provided proof that the preservation of order in Alabama necessitated the presence of Federal troops. On one occasion Perrin rode ahead, out of sight of a company of soldiers, shot a hole in his own hat, and waited for the rest to catch up. Then, shouting that he had been set upon by members of the Ku Klux Klan in ambush, Perin deployed the company as skirmishers against the imaginary enemies. Several Northern papers reported this incident as a "Southern outrage" and the government in Washington felt satisfied that such events required the continued presence of troops in Alabama.[81]

UNION LEAGUE CRIMES, NOT KLAN

Editor Ryland Randolph of *The Tuscaloosa Independent Monitor* wrote in September 1869 that "carpetbag incendiaries [Union Leaguers] are roaming through the northern counties of the state claiming to be the Ku Klux, as to make capital for their party as well as to rob blacks and have the deeds laid on respectable whites. None of the outrages that are now committed are the works of the so-called Ku Kluxes."

Albion Tourgee, the famous carpetbagger Supreme Court judge in North Carolina, wrote that the Ku Klux had broken into 4,000 to 5,000 houses, burned 14, and murdered 13 in one county. Later he said he was misquoted:

51

I wrote 4 arsons instead of 14. Instead of 4 to 5,000 houses opened, I wrote 4-500. I said 13 murders in the state, not in the district." Still later it was found that the house burnings were perpetrated by Governor Holden's Union League militia to provoke resistance to the Klan.[82]

---

[78] Horn, p. 2.

[79] Fernando Wood, "Alleged Ku Klux Outrages," speech in The United States House of Representatives, 30 March 1871 (Washington: Congressional Globe Printing Office, 1871), p. 5.

[80] William H. Smith, "Radical Falsehoods Exposed," extracts of a letter (Washington: National Democratic Executive Committee, 1870.)

[81] *The Alabama Review*, Vol. XV, No. 2, April 1962, p. 140.

[82] Horn, pp. 140 and 200.

THE "FORCE LAWS":

UNCONSTITUTIONAL FEDERAL TERROR

THE "FORCE LAWS" were conceived to "enforce the provisions of the 14th Amendment" and were the consequence of the Congressional Ku Klux Klan committee's work and the false reports it generated.

The resolution for enacting the Force Law (Enforcement Law) was read by Senator Sherman of Ohio:

Resolved: that the Ku Klux Klan, as it is called under various names, is now a formidable military power in 11 states of this Union, is shown by all contemporaneous history, as well as by the sworn proof of great numbers of witnesses given before one of the committees of this body. Resolved: That as organised bands of desperate and lawless men, disciplined and disguised, and bound by oaths and secret organisations, have, by terror, and violence, subverted all civil authority in large parts of the late insurrectionary states, thus utterly overthrowing the safety of persons and property, and all those rights which are the primary basis and object of all civil government, and which are expressly guaranteed by the Constitution of the United States to all its citizens; and as the courts are rendered utterly powerless by organised perjury, to punish crime, therefore the Judiciary Committee is instructed to report a bill that will enable the President and the courts of the United States to execute the laws, punish organised violence, and secure to all citizens so guaranteed to them.[83]

In response to this resolution, Senator Bayard of Delaware (later appointed Secretary of State by President Grover Cleveland) made a speech condemning the resolution:

> Sir, this resolution is unprecedented in the history of this government in the violence of its language and the reckless indefiniteness of its assertions. It specified no man, no state or any part of a state. It is a broadcast charge, totally without those elements of certainty which are held necessary to charge the humblest man with the smallest offense known to our criminal laws ... what then, is its origin? Is it not the voice of a secret conclave of party, without the safeguards of open discussion, without any of the safeguards which the rules of evidence throws around every man and every community for their protection ... when legislation in a body constituted as this is to have its efficient creation in a secret party caucus, we are little better off than in those dark days of Venetian history when the Council of Ten sat in secret and the accusations anonymously made were thrown into the mouth of the bronze lion, standing ready to receive them.[84]

The former mayor of New York City, Fernando Wood, also spoke against the Enforcement Act when he became a Congressman:

> I hope to speak temperately, dispassionately, and calmly ... I can scarcely believe that so radical a revolution has overcome the institutions of this country, that a committee of the House will formally and seriously propose legislation of this character. I can scarcely realise that within the short period of

54

10 or 12 years political sentiment on the other side [Republicans] has become so radical as to countenance a serious proposition in the House of Representatives to create a military despotism on the ruins of the Republic .... [It contains] the very essence of despotism, the very concentration of imperial irresponsible power to be placed in the hands of one man, to create here at the capital of our country a military chieftain ... this power is to be placed in the hands of a layman, the present President [Grant]. It does appear that the second section [of the law] which declares that two or more persons will constitute what is called in the third section, "an unlawful combination," and according to the 4th section, that unlawful combination, authorises the President of the United States, when in his judgment, it will be required, to suspend the privileges of habeas corpus and to declare and enforce martial law, subject to the rules and articles of war, and other laws now in force applicable in case of rebellion ... In no portion of our history has any such authority been delegated; in no free government anywhere in the world has any such power been delegated by the people, nor is there any despot for the past century who would attempt to exercise it. Napoleon, in the day of his imperial strength, never attempted to exercise it; and not even the life of the present Emperor of Russia, with all his great personal authority, holding in his hands not only the church but the state, not only the sword but the purse, whose subjects are vassals, would feel safe for 24 hours if he attempted to exercise the power now proposed to be given to the President of the United States.[85]

[83] Bayard, p. 1.

[84] *Ibid.*, p. 2.

[85] Wood, p. 2.

CONCLUSION 1: THE CONSEQUENCES

OF THE UNION LEAGUE FOR NOW

THE HISTORIAN of the Georgia Union League aptly summarises the legacy of the League:

> The prejudices and antagonisms that the Union League fostered are felt even to this day. It is obvious that if the building tendencies of the days just following the war had been cultivated and allowed to take their course, the problem of the black freedmen would have slowly evolved a solution. For by and large, the white men of the state [Georgia] were sincerely and seriously interested in the welfare of the black ...

> The Union League of Georgia did more to breed suspicion between the races, to create misunderstanding, to ignite often justifiably but none the less dangerous explosions of feeling and conduct, to estrange the black man from the people among whom he must live, to fan alive and to kindle in new places fires of prejudice, than any other single influence. There can be no doubt that if the races had not been set against each other, these situations pregnant with fearful implications for the future, would never have come about ...

> The Union League distorted the black's reaction to freedom, enslaved him politically for a time, and was a vital factor in creating the situations that have resulted in his economic slavery.[86]

[86] Cason, p. 153.

CONCLUSION 2: DECLINE IN MORALITY

DUE TO UNION LEAGUE

DR. HENRY BELLOWS, founder of the Union League, demonstrated the inescapable consequences of the violence and corruption in the South for the Northern states:

There was something more hopeless and desperate in the political, social and commercial demoralisation that followed the war than in the war itself. That presented an open enemy, whom powder and shot could reach and overcome; but we had in place of this a secret rot, an enemy with the inviolable power of a pestilence, in which the old and pestilent doctrine of the spoils to the victors had changed from an acknowledged heresy into a dogma, not so much adopted, as incarnate in the life of the parties.

This is inevitably due to the pillaging corruption of the carpetbag Republicans in the South, which spread to the North as well. Bellows continues:

Nothing less than a moral typhoid, the consequence of a general malaria in the public air, can account for the sinking tone of public sentiment during the decade following the close of the war; partly a reaction to the exalted patriotism that had sustained the war into victory, partly the dreadful result of the unsettling influence on values, standards, habits, by the creation of an artificial currency that did not carry its measure in itself, partly by the coming to the top of powerful men who had suddenly become rich without the aid of any moral habit or any refined or gentlemanly standards.

Dr. Bellows is railing against the very things he fanatically strove to achieve in the South: a new social order which required destroying their moral and cultural standards. The intensity of the effort consumed the whole nation. The immoral wealth-getting of the carpetbaggers was considered a high morality as long as it was confined to plundering the hated, defeated enemy. It seemed different and shocking only when these kinds of men and these values visited Northern doorsteps:

Vikings in energy, unscrupulousness and violence, who swept through the land in railroad land grabs, in mining speculations, in purchase of legislatures, in stock dilutions, in great corners on stock and grain, and who intoxicated and poisoned the once sober blood of the people, until politics had become a trade, or a gambling shop, a trial of wits, or a turn of chance.

All these supposed negatives were treated as wonderful positives as long as they remained the standard way of doing business in the South. In conclusion, says Bellows,

A profound distrust of American principles and ideas came over the better part of Europe, as it witnessed this consequence of the war which had an end so different from their predictions and hopes. How a nation that had surprised Europe with its patriotism and its patience after victory, could surprise it again with its disgusting loss of moral control in its great centers, its rings, and its legislative and aldermanic vileness, corruption and vulgarity, and all within a single decade, were as disheartening at home, and as secretly demoralising even to the better half of the American people, as it was taunting and distressing to those who went abroad and bore the ignominy of almost universal ridicule and distrust. This decline in the public tone was not confined to the vulgar and the ignorant. It affected all ranks and professions, perhaps most marked where it would naturally be least looked for, and most abhorrent, in the clerical calling. No doubt it affected injuriously many of the leaders of all parties and every school of politics, the Senate, the Bench, the Bar.[87]

---

[87] Bellows, pp. 123-125.

ABOUT THE AUTHOR

JOHN CHODES is a playwright, biographer, and historian. His books include, among others, *The Myth of America's Military Power (1972); Corbitt: The Story of Ted Corbitt, Long Distance Runner* (1973), which won the "Journalistic Excellence Award" from the Road Runners Club of America; *Bruce Jenner* (1976), which has sold over 200,000 copies; *Destroying the Republic: Jabez Curry and the Re-education of the Old South* (2005); *Horatio Seymour: New York's Governor Attacks Abe Lincoln's War* (2011); *In Praise of the Free Market and Peace* (2012); and *Abe Lincoln's Secret War Against the North* (2012).

Mr. Chodes has published more than 100 articles in various books and journals (including *Chronicles, The Freeman, Social Justice Review, The New York Tribune* and others). He was technical advisor for the movie "Marathon Man." He was Communications Director for the New York Libertarian Party for which he received an award for Meritorious Service. His greatest distinction perhaps is as a dramatist. Eight of his plays, mostly on historical subjects, have been produced off-Broadway.

A lifelong resident of New York, Mr. Chodes became interested in the history of the War Between the States and the South when he looked into the U.S. Army invasion and occupation of his city during that war. He writes that he is interested in free trade, limited government, the privatisation of education, and a deregulated economy---principles of the Old South.

AVAILABLE FROM SHOTWELL

PUBLISHING

When the Yankees Come: Former South Carolina Slaves Remember Sherman's Invasion. Edited with Introduction by Paul C. Graham (2016)

Southerner, Take Your Stand! by John Vinson *(2016)*

Lies My Teacher Told Me: The True History of the War for Southern Independence by Clyde N. Wilson (2016)

Emancipation Hell: The Tragedy Wrought By Lincoln's Emancipation Proclamation by Kirkpatrick Sale (2015)

Southern Independence. Why War? - The War to Prevent Southern Independence by Dr. Charles T. Pace (2015)

For More Information, Visit us Online at
WWW.SHOTWELLPUBLISHING.COM

CPSIA information can be obtained at www.ICGtesting.com
Printed in the USA
LVOW10s1423270516

490291LV00015B/126/P